George Washington Carleton

**Our artist in Cuba**

Fifty drawings on wood

George Washington Carleton

**Our artist in Cuba**
*Fifty drawings on wood*

ISBN/EAN: 9783337258764

Printed in Europe, USA, Canada, Australia, Japan

Cover: Foto ©Thomas Meinert / pixelio.de

More available books at **www.hansebooks.com**

# OUR

# ARTIST IN CUBA.

## FIFTY DRAWINGS ON WOOD.

LEAVES FROM

### THE SKETCH-BOOK OF A TRAVELER,

DURING THE WINTER OF 1864-5.

BY

### GEO. W. CARLETON.

NEW YORK:

*Carleton, Publisher,* 413 *Broadway.*

London: *S. Low, Son & Co.*

MDCLXV.

# CONTENTS.

A PRELIMINARY WORD.

# A PRELIMINARY WORD.

WITH many misgivings, the author of this little *brochure* has been persuaded to give the prominence of publication to a mere pocket-book collection of way-side pen-and-ink sketches, the chance results of idle moments, sandwiched with such Cuban events as paring oranges and sipping from their cups of nectar—tearing through the narrow streets of Havana in ragged volantes—listening in the soft moonlight, and arm-in-arm with Cuban señoritas, to the Artillery band in the Plaza des Armas—assisting with domino and false nose at the masquerades in the Tacon Theatre — lounging with ices or delicious chocolate at the Café Dominica — dallying with cigar and fragrant coffee, after the regulation breakfast of codfish, garlic, and onions — snuffing up the perfumed air,

and strolling through the golden orange-
groves of Cafetals — joining in the battle,
murder, and sudden death of Marinao cock-
fights — vagabondizing along the shady side
of Calle Obispo—and so forth, through all
the *dolce far nientes* of a stranger's drift-
ing life, among the lights and shadows of
the Antilles' Queen.

The only merit the pictures possess,
perhaps, is their faithfulness to nature.
Though chiefly caricatures, they represent
such incidents and scenes as every one,
with both eyes open, sees, who visits Cuba ;
and being sketched upon the spot, with all
the crispy freshness of a first impression,
they possess a sort of photographic value,
that, in spite of their grotesqueness, may
prove more lasting than the entertainment
which their humor offers.

New York, April, 1865.

First day out.—The wind freshens up a trifle as we get outside Sandy Hook; but our artist says he is 'nt sea-sick, for he never felt better in his life.

A " Booby "—as seen *from* the ship's deck.

A Booby—as seen *on* the ship's deck.

# ARRIVAL AT HAVANA.

A side elevation of the colored gentleman who carried
our luggage from the small boat to the Custom House.

The first volante driver that our artist saw in Havana.

The old Convent and Bell Tower of the Church
of San Francisco,—now used as a Custom House.

STREETS OF HAVANA.—CALLE TENIENTE RE.

A Cuban Cart and its Motive Power.—Ye patient Donkey.

Manners and Customs of a Cuban with
a Cold in his Head.

I.

II.

PART I.—The beast in a torpid condition.

PART II.—When he "smells the blood of an Englishmun."

THE NATIONAL VEHICLE OF HAVANA.

Manner and Custom of Harnessing ye Animiles to ye Cuban Volante.

9

I.—Chanticleer as he goes in.

II.—Chanticleer considerably "played out."

The cool and airy style in which they dress
the rising colored generation of Havana.

THE CUBAN TOOTH-PICK.

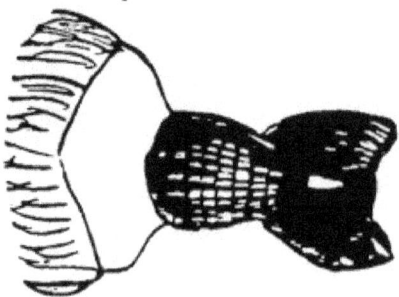

"Two ways of carrying it—behind the ear, and in the back-hair.

# THE CAPTAIN GENERAL'S QUINTA.

View of the Canal and Cocoa Tree ; looking East
from the Grotto.

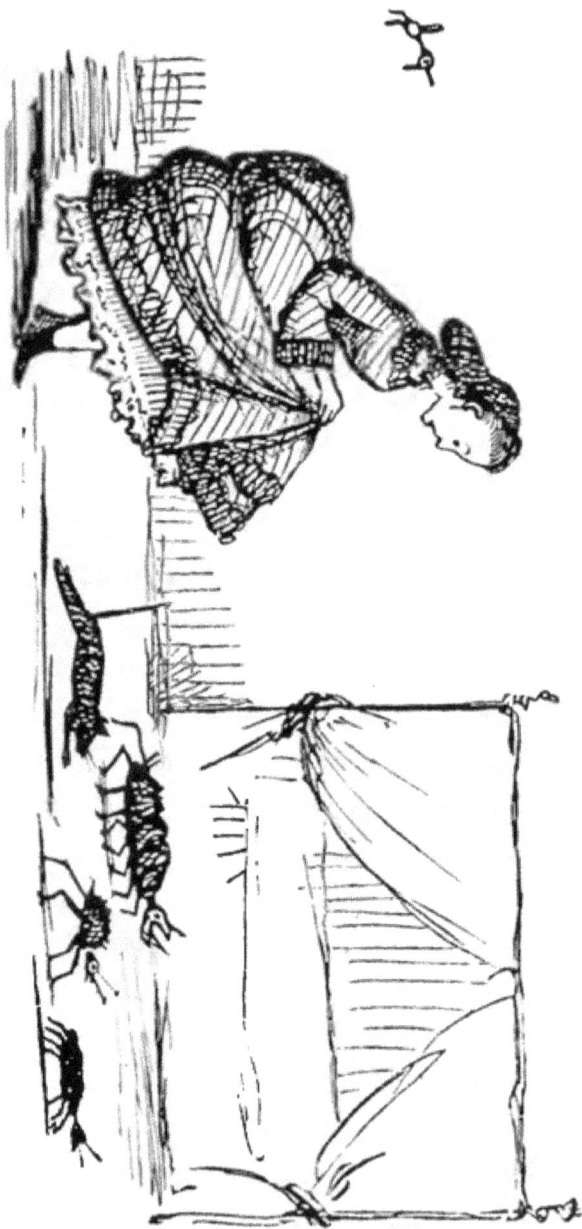

THE DOMESTIC INSECTS OF HAVANA.

Agitation of the Better-Half of Our Artist, upon entering her chamber and making their acquaintance.

# A LITTLE EPISODE IN THE CALLE BARRATILLO.

A slight difference arises between the housekeeper's cat and the butcher's dog, who has just come out in his summer costume.

The Free Negro.—An everyday scene, when
the weather is fine.

Kitchen, chief-cook and bottle-washer in the establishment of Mrs. Franke, out on the "Cerro."

A portrait of the young lady, whose family (after considerable urging) consents to take in our washing.

PRIMITIVE HABITS OF THE NATIVES.

Washing in Havana.—$4 ∞ a dozen in gold

I.—My pantaloons as they went *in*.   II.—My pantaloons as they came *out*.

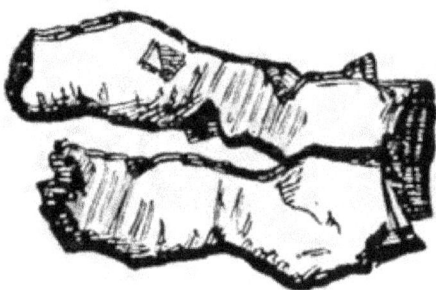

CARNIVAL IN HAVANA.

A Masquerade at the Tacon Theatre.—Types of Costume, with a glimpse of the "Cuban Dance" in the background.

Our artist mixes in the giddy dance, and falls
desperately in love with this sweet creature——but

When the "sweet creature" unmasks, our Artist
suddenly recovers from his fit of admiration.   Alas!
beauty is but mask deep.

23

STREETS OF HAVANA—CALLE OBRAPIA.

The Cuban Wheelbarrow—In Repose.

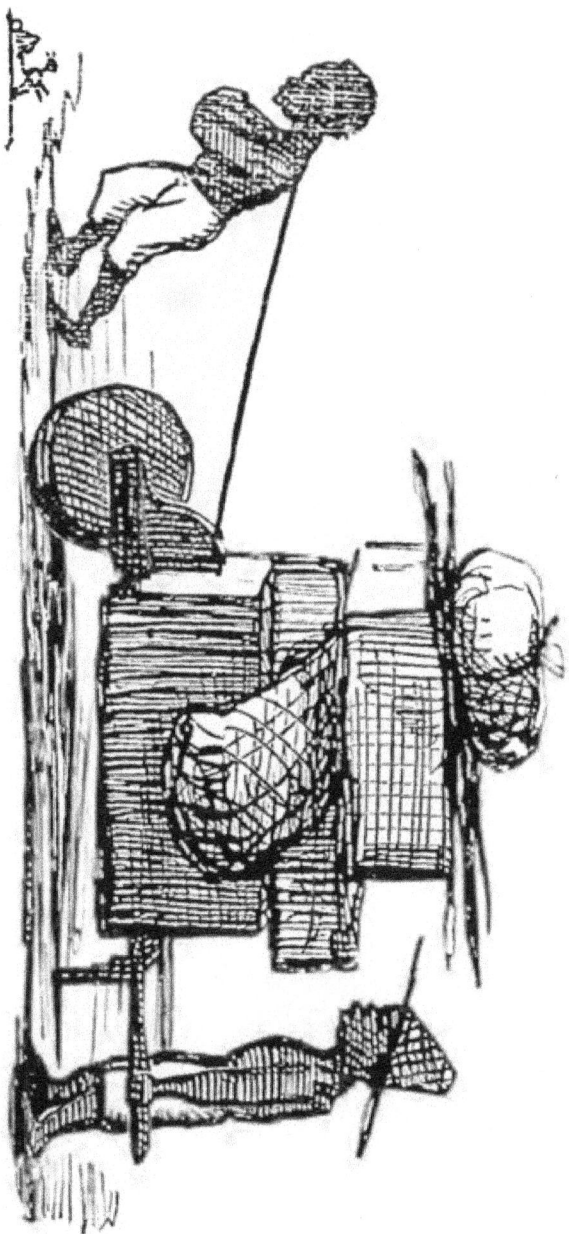

STREETS OF HAVANA—CALLE O'REILLY.

The Cuban Wheelbarrow—In action.

## FIRST HOUR I

## SECOND HOUR II

## THIRD HOUR III

Our Artist forms the praiseworthy determination of studying the Spanish language, and devotes three hours to the enterprise.

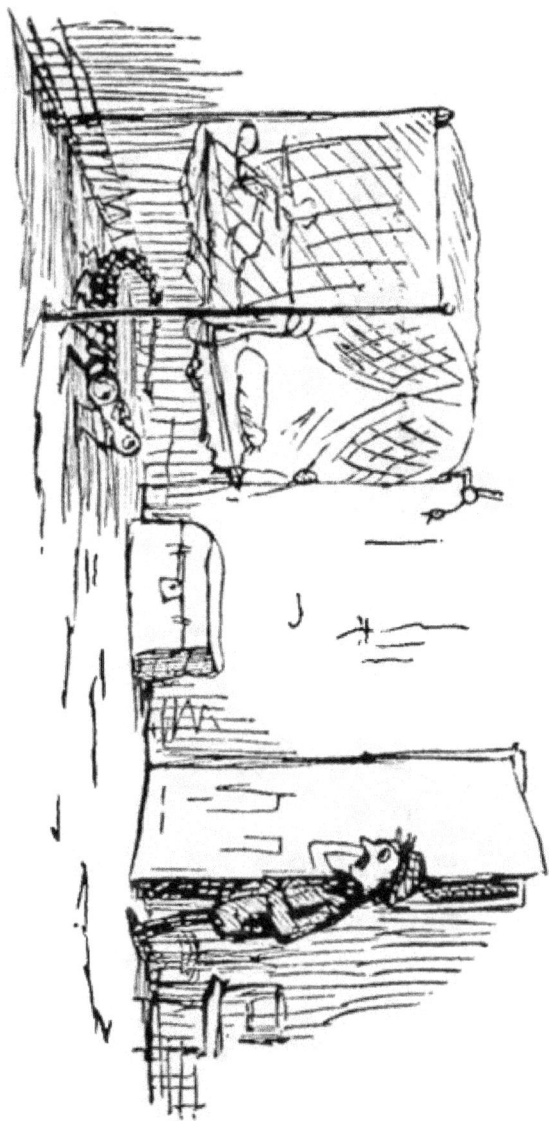

BED-ROOMS IN CUBA.

'The Scorpion of Havana,—encountered in his native jungle.

Our Artist having prepared himself for a jolly plunge, inadvertently observes an insect peculiar to the water, and rather thinks he won't go in just now.

A cheerful Chinese Chambermaid (?) at the
Fonda de Ingleterra, outside the walls.

A gay (but slightly mutilated) old plaster-of-Paris girl, that I found in one of the avenues of the Bishop's Garden, on the " Cerro."

30

LOCOMOTION IN THE COUNTRY.

A Cuban Planter going into town with his plunder.

RESULT!

Our Artist just steps around the corner, to look at a "sweet thing in fans" that his wife has found.

## THE NATIONAL BEVERAGE OF HAVANA.

Our Artist indulges in a *panale frio* (a sort of lime-ade), at the Café Donnica, and gets so "set up," that he vows he won't go home till morning.

THE LIZARDS OF CUBA.

Our Artist, on an entomological expedition in the Bishop's Garden, is disagreeably surprised to find such sprightly specimens.

34

SMOKING IN HAVANA.

An English acquaintance of Our Artist wants a light for his paper segar ; whereupon the waiter, according to custom, brings a live coal.

35

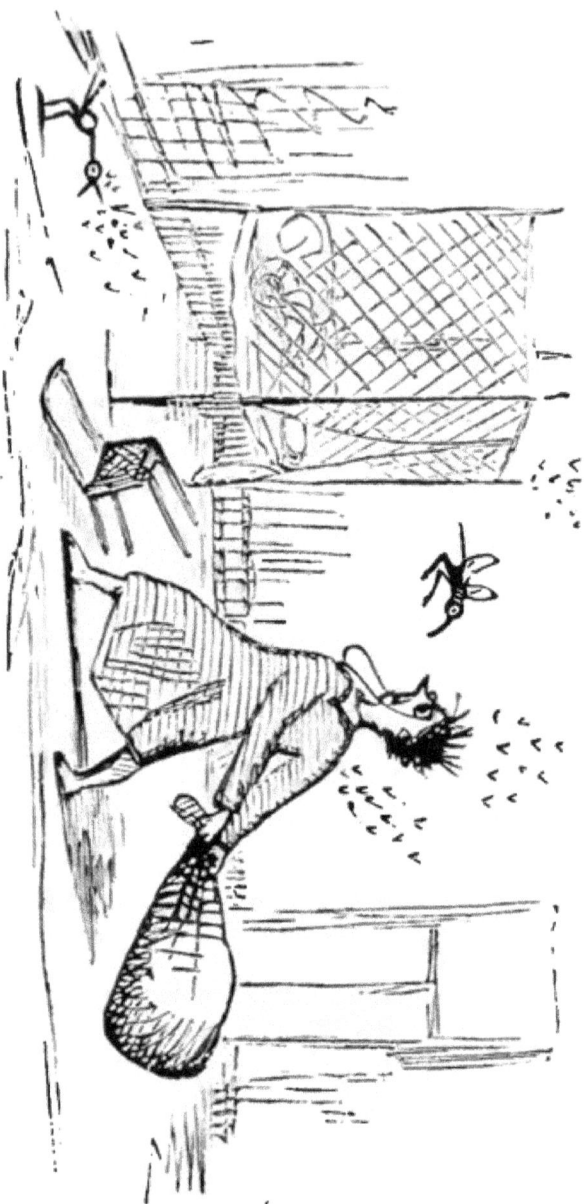

A midsummer's night dream.—Our Artist is just the least bit disturbed in his rest, and gently remonstrates.

A gay and festive Chinese brakeman, on the railroad near Guines.—The shirt-collar-and-pair-of-spurs style of costume.

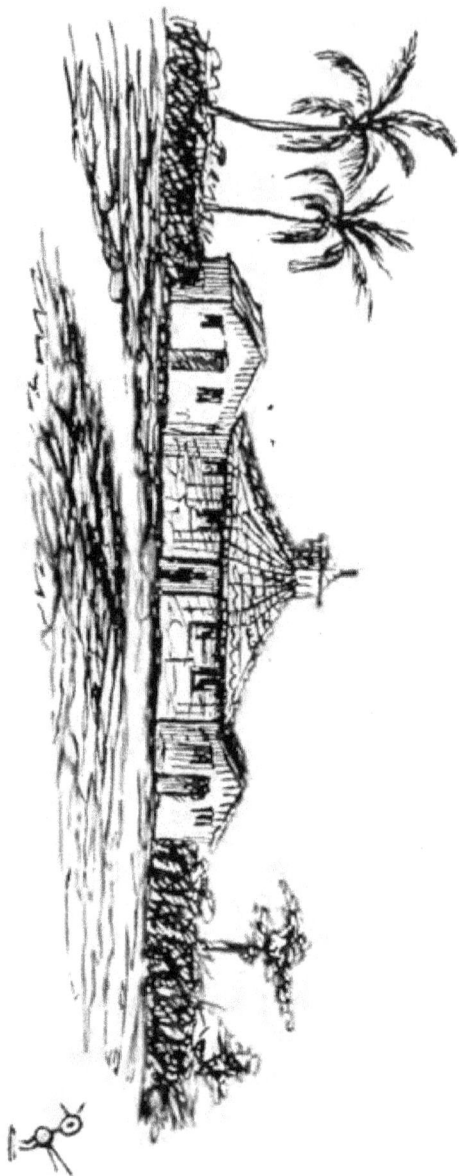

ONE OF THE SENSATIONS IN CUBA.

The Great Cave near Matanzas.—Picturesque House over the Entrance.

THE GREAT CAVE NEAR MATANZAS.

A section of the interior—showing the comfortable manner in which our artist followed the guide, inspected the stalactites, and comported himself generally.

39

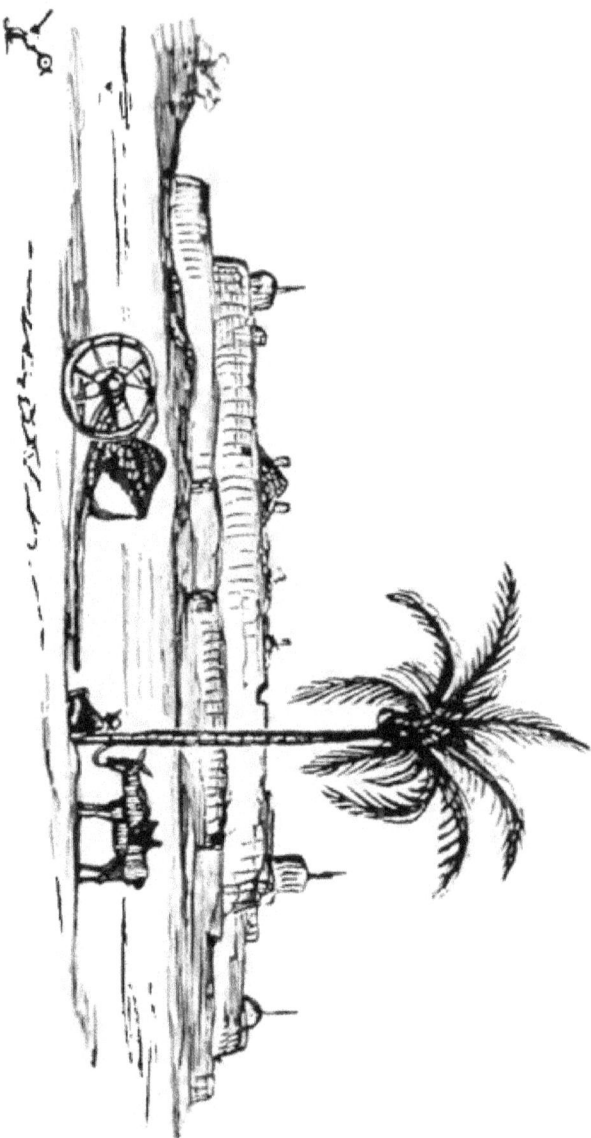

One of the Fortifications.—Sketched from the end of the *Passeo*, on a day hot enough to give anything but a donkey the brain fever.

A romantic little *tienda mista* (grocery store) on a corner, in the Calle Ona.

A CAFFETAL NEAR MATANZAS.

Our Artist becomes dumb with admiration, at the ingenious manner of toting little niggers.

THE PICTURESQUE IN MATANZAS.

A singular little bit, out of the Calle Manzana.

43

A SUGAR PLANTATION, NEAR THE YUMORI.

Our Artist essays to drink the milk from a green Cocoa:

Fatal effect.—An uncomfortable sensation!

A BED-CHAMBER IN MATANZAS.

First night at the "Gran Hotel Leon de Oro."—Our artist is accommodated with quarters on the ground-floor, convenient to the court-yard, and is lulled to sleep by a little domestic concert of cats, dogs, donkeys, parrots and game-cocks.

Showing the manner in which one ox accomplishes the labor of two, in San Felipe.

46

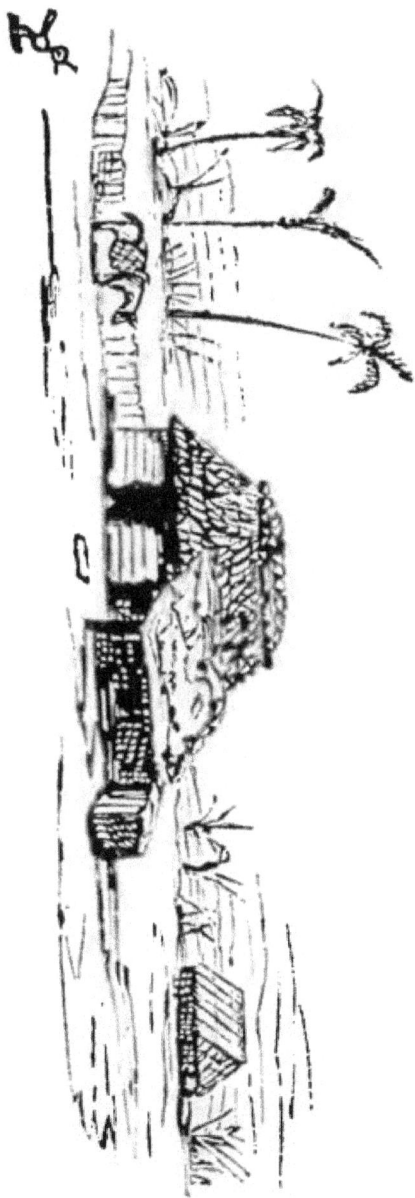

THE SUBURBS OF CALABAZAR

A Planter's Hut, and three scraggly Palm Trees in the dim distance.

A Colored Beauty toting Sugar Cane from the field to the grinding mill.

A conglomerate *Esquiria*, on the corner of Calle Obispo and Monserate.

Alarm of Our Artist and Wife, upon going to their room to pack, and discovering that a Tarantula has taken possession of their trunk.

*9 7 8 3 3 3 7 2 5 8 7 6 4 *